ROCK POOLS AND SEASHELLS

Along the South Hams' Coastline

© Bryan Ashby and Gordon Waterhouse

ORCHARD PUBLICATIONS
2 Orchard Close, Chudleigh, Newton Abbot, Devon TQ13 0LR
Telephone: 01626 852714

ISBN   9781898964834

Printed by Hedgerow Print
Crediton, Devon EX17 1ES

i

CONTENTS

The Beaches of the South Hams 1

The Tideline – Flotsam and Jetsam 2

Walking down the Shore 6

Rock Pools 14

The Lower Shore – Gullies and Boulders 21

Shell Collecting – Art and Games 32

Seaweeds 34

THE BEACHES OF
THE SOUTH HAMS

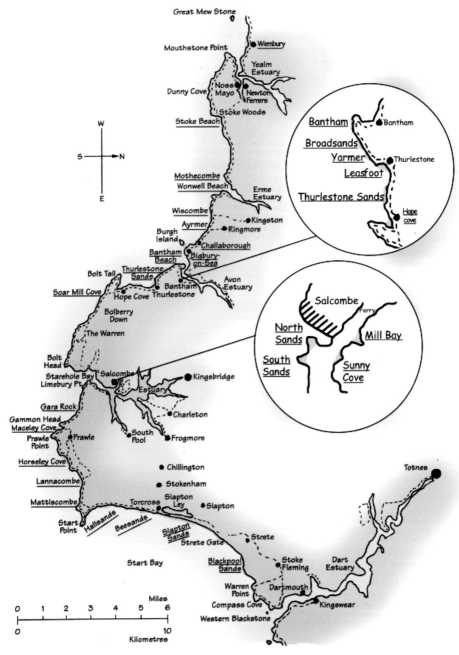

Great Mew Stone

Mouthstone Point

Wembury

Yealm Estuary

Dunny Cove · Noss Mayo · Newton Ferrers

Stoke Woods

Stoke Beach

Mothecombe
Wonwell Beach

Erme Estuary

Wiscombe

Ayrmer · Kingston

Burgh Island · Ringmore

Challaborough

Bantham Beach · Bigbury-on-Sea

Bolt Tail

Thurlestone Sands

Avon Estuary

Soar Mill Cove

Bantham Thurlestone

Hope Cove Thurlestone

Bolberry Down

The Warren

Bolt Head

Starehole Bay · Salcombe
Limebury Pt.

Estuary · Kingsbridge

Gara Rock

Gammon Head
Maceley Cove

Charleton

Prawle Point · Prawle

South Pool · Frogmore

Horseley Cove

Chillington

Lannacombe

Stokenham

Mattiscombe

Torcross

Slapton Ley · Slapton

Start Point · Hallsands · Beesands

Slapton Sands

Strete Gate · Strete

Start Bay

Blackpool Sands

Stoke Fleming

Dart Estuary

Totnes

Warren Point · Dartmouth

Compass Cove · Kingswear

Western Blackstone

W
S → N
E

(inset circle, top right)
__Bantham__
__Broadsands__
__Yarmer__
__Leasfoot__
__Thurlestone Sands__

Bantham

Thurlestone

Hope cove

(inset circle, middle right)
Salcombe
Ferry

North Sands

Mill Bay

South Sands

Sunny Cove

Miles
0 1 2 3 4 5 6

0   10
Kilometres

1

Beach and tideline at Bantham

Seaweeds, litter and a fascinating mixture of animal remains – hints of earlier and other creation – are left by the sea, along the tideline. There are mermaids' purses; brown pouches with curling tendrils at each corner belong to dogfish and black pouches with long points at each corner belong to rays, most commonly the thornback ray. Inside the mermaid's purse a single fish develops until it is mature enough to swim away. White, oval 'bones' are the internal skeletons of cuttlefish – strange, fish-like molluscs that prey on crustaceans and hide from predators in a puff of sepia smoke of their own making. What appear to be bath sponges made of papery bubbles are groups of whelk egg-cases. Inside each bubble were about twenty eggs. The first to hatch eat the remaining eggs before drifting off into the

Dog fish purse

plankton. Lobed fronds of what apears to be a dried, buff-seaweed are colonies of animals - bryozoa or 'moss animals'– called hornrack. (see p 33)

Dead and dying jellyfish and their allies lie among the flotsam and jetsam. The transparent, common jellyfish have four violet rings at their centre. The larger, compass jellyfish have brown lines dividing the circular body into segments, like a compass rose, and brown dots around the circumference. They have many, fine tentacles and four, long, trailing ones that sting and earn it the name of sea nettle.

By-the-wind-sailors

Compass jellyfish

Transparent, rigid ovals with a half-moon sail are by-the-wind-sailors. At first sight they look as if they are made of colourless plastic. Sometimes the blue tentacles still survive, showing them to be relatives of the jellyfish.

All the jellyfish clan use their tentacles to ensnare and paralyse the plankton, on which they feed. By-the-wind-sailors are blown across the Atlantic and are occasionally washed up in their thousands. You may be lucky enough to find the shell of the violet snail, round and violet coloured. They float in a life-jacket of bubbles along with the by-the-wind-sailors which they eat as they drift across the ocean.

After the autumn gales, goose barnacles may be washed up; dozens of them hanging from pieces of plastic or driftwood. These barnacles, with long, black 'necks' capped by overlapping, white plates, have also been blown to our shores from the Atlantic Ocean. In Mediaeval times it was thought that the geese with black necks and heads patterned with white, that came each autumn to Northern Ireland and Western Scotland, hatched from goose barnacles. Huge flocks still come there each winter and to this day they are called barnacle geese.

On the tideline above sandy shores, sea potatoes are often washed up – they are the brittle, white shells (about the size of a misshapen table tennis ball) of a sea urchin that lives beneath the sand.

Cuttlefish 'bone'. Ray's 'purse'. Whelk eggcases.

Goose barnacles

Goose barnacle, showing feeding net

Under the flotsam and jetsam, especially under the line of rotting seaweed, live thousands of sandhoppers. The family of sandhoppers (side-shrimps) , with sideways-flattened bodies, belong to the order of amphipods (Greek for 'feet on both sides') in the great class of crustaceans, which includes barnacles, prawns, lobsters and crabs.

Grey-brown, sparrow-sized birds pecking along the tide-line for sandhoppers will be rock pipits; they have grey-white outer tail feathers. Wagtails too feed along the tideline – our resident pied wagtails and migrant white wagtails from Iceland. They are so alike it is impossible for most of us to tell them apart. Migrating wading birds also come, many of them on their way between breeding grounds in Scotland or Iceland and wintering territories on the estuaries and coasts of southern Europe or North Africa.

Mating sandhoppers

Turnstones, their orange legs scampering over the stranded seaweed, walk along the tideline flicking over the stones or seaweed and snapping up the sandhoppers underneath. The other waders – flocks of dunlin, sanderling and some ringed

4

Rock pipit

plover – poke their beaks into the soft sand to find sandhoppers and other burrowing shrimps. In April and May there may also be whimbrel, the small cousin of the curlew.

Plastic, including discarded fishing net and line, is the life-threatening scourge we have added to the flotsam and jetsam of the tideline. A positive contribution would be if each of us, at the end of our day's rockpooling, were to collect up some in a bag and take it home to dispose of safely.

"Too big for us to turn" , say these turnstones

Sanderling

5

WALKING DOWN THE SHORE

Mattiscombe Beach and Prawle Point

As the tide begins to ebb, we can begin to explore the world between the tides. Wear a pair of old trainers or something similar – don't go in bare feet, the rocks and barnacles can cut them. Take a net, preferably with a straight bottom edge, a light coloured bowl into which you can put your catches and a magnifying glass to look more closely at the smaller creatures.

The shore can be divided into four zones; first the splash zone which may be splashed by the waves but only actually covered by water at high 'spring tides', then the upper shore, middle shore and finally lower shore, which is only uncovered at low water 'spring tides'.

Above the splash zone are lichens, grey ones above orange ones and smooth black lichen, like a band of tar around high tide mark. At the lower end of this band are bushy tufts of another black lichen *Lichina pygmaea*.

Look carefully at the bare rock in the splash zone. In the narrow cracks live

Grey, orange and black lichens on rock

thousands of sea slaters and bristletails, which come out at night and scavenge, – the cleaning service of the splash zone. Sea slaters are related to woodlice and are in the order of isopods (Greek for 'equal feet') which, like the sandhoppers, are crustaceans. The bristletails are primitive insects with long, tapering bodies and a three pronged tail.

In these same cracks, especially on rocks exposed to the south-west, where the waves splash up highest, are clustered groups of small winkles, no bigger than

Sea slater

grape pips and the colour of purple grapes. Below this level, the cracks are full of slightly bigger winkles - rough winkles - whose shells are grooved like an old fashioned gramophone record – the more exposed the shore the deeper the grooves in the rough winkles' shells. They vary in colour from grey to orange-yellow.

Barnacles give a grey-white speckling to the bare rock of the upper and middle shore. Although they resemble miniature limpets, they are crustaceans, not molluscs.

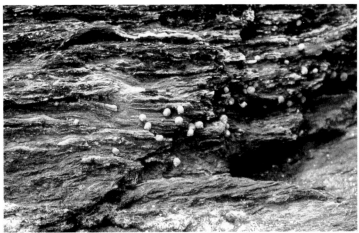
Rough winkles and black lichen on rock in the splash zone

They begin their lives floating in the plankton, looking very like the planktonic stage of shore crabs. Later, they glue themselves, head downwards, to the bare rock and live out their lives sweeping for microscopic plankton with their feathery 'legs', when the tide comes in. Barnacles higher on the shore are mostly *Chthamalus*, which tend to have a kite-shaped opening at the top. From the middle shore most of the barnacles are *Semibalanus*, which have a diamond shaped opening at the top. Inside dead barnacles, rough winkles and other small molluscs often make a home.

Chthamalus barnacles and black lichen

On the lower shore, especially in shaded overhangs, are scattered individuals of a volcano-shaped species of barnacle, called *Balanus perforatus*.

Larger than barnacles, like Chinamen's hats stuck to the rock, are limpets. These shellfish rasp the algal slime from the rock as they trail over the rock at high tide, returning to their home patch as the tide begins to fall. So faithfully do they return to exactly the same spot each time, that they wear away a ring in the rock, where their shell clamps down. Many winkles and topshells live about ten years but limpets can survive for fifteen or more.

Dog-whelks, off-white molluscs with pointed shells, are often found near

Limpet homes past and present. Pepper dulse growing in the centre.
Purple rock-weed Lithothamnia spreading over the rock

barnacles and limpets. They rasp away at the protective shells of barnacles and limpets, to make a hole through which they suck out the insides. Another mollusc found on the bare rock in a narrow band around the upper to middle shore is the thick topshell (also sometimes called the toothed winkle, as it has a white bump, like a tooth, around the opening curve of the shell).

Dog whelk attacking limpet   *Thick topshell and flat winkles*

Following the tide's retreat, where the exposure to the waves is not too severe, there are zones of seaweeds growing on the rock: first a narrow zone of channel wrack, followed by a wider one of spiral wrack, then a very wide zone of knotted wrack. Knotted wrack has big, single bladders down the stem. At the edge of the knotted wrack there may be some bladder wrack, which has pairs of smaller bladders. Last of the wracks, down by the lower shore, is the saw wrack, with its edge serrated like a saw blade.

Channel wrack

Spiral wrack

Knotted wrack

Zones of seaweed

Other creatures and plants may be attached to the wracks. Sea-firs are some of the most abundant – a forest of grey stems with many short projections, branching out like a herring-bone. They are animals not plants. From the projections bud medusae, resembling anemones or jellyfish. Some of the anemone-like buds are a delicate pink.

Attached to the knotted wrack are tufts of a dark red, almost black, seaweed, *Polysiphonia*, that only grows on knotted wrack.

Flat winkles – yellow, green, orange or brown - browse on these wracks and are beautifully camouflaged like extra bladders on the fronds.

Channel wrack with barnacle and black lichen

Spiral wrack

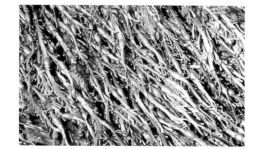

Knotted wrack

Especially on the saw wrack, tiny, many white whorls are stuck to the seaweed. These chalky tubes are the homes of spiral tube-worms. Longer, snaky white tubes are the homes of serpent tube-worms both these tube-worms are also found on rock.

Polysiphonia on knotted wrack with fruiting 'raisins'

Flat winkles on knotted wrack

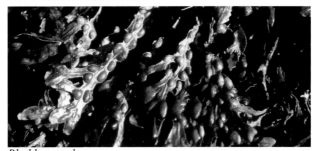

Bladder wrack

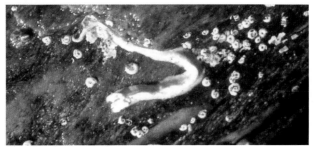

Spiral and serpent tube-worms

Where the knotted or saw-wracks overhang rocky gullies in thick curtains, a swish of the curtain will reveal a wonder-world. Bright orange and pale green sponges spread over the wet rock and weep water at a touch. Deep red beadlet anemones and green spotted strawberry anemones hang, as drooping rubbery bulbs, their tentacles withdrawn inside. Various small, red seaweeds – flat tongues, ferny branches, strings of sausages, even soft pink drapes with white bags attached, which are purse sponges – all hang from the rock as a beautiful tapestry. Let go the slimy curtain of wracks and the magical world is completely hidden again.

A wonder-world of sponges and anemones

Green breadcrumb sponge, purple rock-weed and on left carragheen moss (Chondrus crispus)

Beadlet anemone

Sheets of what appears to be brown-black or purple-black clingfilm sometimes cover the bare rock. This weed is boiled and eaten in parts of Wales, as laverbread. Carragheen 'mosses' are also edible. These branched, dark purplish weeds, only a few centimetres high, grow in cracks in the bare rock or round the edge of rock pools on the middle and lower shore. Caragheen mosses are eaten as a delicacy with potatoes in Ireland. An even smaller weed, pepper dulse, grows in similar places, and has a sharp, peppery taste. It is branched like a small fern and although usually dark purple, where it is exposed to more sunlight, it turns greenish-yellow.

Strawberry anemone

Purse sponges on red <u>Plumaria</u> weed. Bottom left, carragheen moss (<u>Mastocarpus</u>)

ROCK POOLS

In hollows in the rocky platforms and gullies are rock pools; they can be big enough for a giant's bath or as small as a fairy's wash basin. Each rock pool is unique but all are colourful oases of beauty.

A rock pool with sea lettuce, coral-weed, bleached purple rock-weed and a beadlet anemone

Most are lined with a pink-purple skin of *Lithothamnia* – purple rock-weed and have bushy tufts of a stiff-branched pink weed, called *Corallina* or coral-weed. Skeleton shrimps, like small, marine stick insects, may sometimes be spotted climbing through the branches of the *Corallina*. In pools, especially on the upper shore, there are green weeds floating up from the purple floor, wide tongues of sea-lettuce and hollow strings of green gut-weed. The dark purple, branching fronds of *Chondrus crispus*, a carragheen moss, are common and a variety of delicate red seaweeds.

Rising high above them, through the still water of pools on the lower shore, there may be green antlers of *Codium* weed (sometimes called velvet horn) or tall bushes of sea-oak or pod-weed (*Halidrys siliquosa*) .

Coral-weed, sea lettuce and saw wrack

Japanese seaweed with green gut-weed

Another interesting weed of the lower shore is the rainbow-weed, which shines iridescently blue, green, yellow and orange in the deeper pools. If you lift it from the water, the colour and the magic vanishes and you are left holding a grey-brown, limp weed.

All these weeds can be smothered by a newcomer, *Sargassum* or Japanese seaweed.This weed was accidentally introduced into France, with Pacific oysters. First found in Britain in 1971, by 1980 it had arrived in the South Hams and it continues to spread northwards.

Rainbow weed

Saw wrack at top, velvet horn central and carragheen moss (Chondrus crispus), bleached pale green at bottom

Swimming through the water and lurking in the weeds are many prawns. You are unlikely to see shrimps in a rock pool. (The best places to find shrimps are in sandy pools. There are some good, big ones at Bantham – good for sailing boats and crawling in, like a crocodile.) The biggest prawns are transparent. One variety, called the chamaeleon prawn, is most common in pools thick with weed; it changes colour to match the weed – green, brown or red. Several types of isopods and amphipods, all smaller than the prawns, can be found swimming in rock pools. A sweep of your net through a weedy pool should catch some of these and lots of prawns.

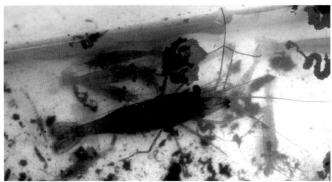

Prawns

Gliding over the rock and its skin of purple rock-weed, in pools from upper to lower shore, are purple topshells, their flattened shells decorated with delicate lines of purple and green, over a pearly background. Thick topshells are also common in pools on the upper and middle shore; they are bigger and less colourful. Edible winkles are another common rock pool mollusc; the shells may become home for a hermit crab, after their original inhabitant has died.

Two Hermit crabs in edible winkle shells

16

From left to right: Small, rough and edible winkles, thick topshell, limpet and dog whelk, flat winkle and purple topshell

Beadlet anemones open their flowers of red tentacles, waiting for any small creatures to venture too close and become ensnared. Buff, purple or green tentacles, belong to snakelocks anemones. The green is an alga which benfits from the anemone and in return produces food by photosynthesis. Snakelocks cannot withdraw their tentacles and so they are always spread out, like Medusa the Gorgon's hair – deadly. Both these anemones reproduce by splitting their bodies and live in clones, members of one clone attacking any incomers with their tentacles.

Beadlet Anemone on bleached purple rock-weed

Snakelocks anemone

17

Another snakelocks anemone in coral-weed

Gem anemones are much less common but may be found near *Corallina* weed. The grey or purple sea-slug feeds on sea anemones, especially beadlets. There are many species of sea-slug specialising on different foods. The sea lemon feeds on sponges. The sea hare looks most like its land-based relatives and is a vegetarian, eating seaweeds; it usually matches the colour of the weeds it is on. The green sea-slug is most often seen on velvet horn, its favourite diet.

Gem anemone (smaller than beadlet and snakelocks anemones

Hiding under overhanging ledges or in dense seaweed are shore crabs, brown, orange or green, scuttling away into a new shelter when disturbed. The very young ones are mottled with white patches, giving a good camouflage.

In corners or crannies of the rock pools or in dense weed, lurk small fish. The common blenny or shanny is the most frequent and may be found at any level of the shore. Montagu's blenny is found mostly in middle shore pools. It has blue spots on its sides and is named after the famous naturalist George Montagu, who lived in Kingsbridge 200 years ago and loved rock pooling and exploring for seashore life. The shores near Thurlestone seem especially good for Montagu's blennies.

Grey sea-slug

Sea lemon sea-slug in carragheen moss (Mastocarpus)

Pair of shore crabs mating

Very young shore crab and flat winkle shell

All blennies have one continuous fin along their backs. Sea scorpions or father lashers, although well camouflaged, have spectacular, spiky fins. Gobies have two separate fins along their back (dorsal fins) and the upper rays of the fins on their sides (pectoral fins) are separate, not joined by a web of skin . Like the blennies, they are found in rock pools. All these fish will eat any small crustacean, including rasping barnacles off the rocks. Living on the surface film of the rockpools there are often clusters of very small, blue springtails. These are one of the very few insects adapted to life between the tides.

Shanny or common blenny

Goby

Horseley Cove at low tide

As the tide sinks to its lowest ebb, a new and most amazing habitat emerges from the sea. Below the zone of saw wrack, whose fronds have jagged edges like a saw blade, rubbery buttons grow. These are the first stage of a remarkable seaweed called thong-weed. Thong-weed is a biennial. In the first year it produces a rubbery button and in the second year a long, khaki-yellow thong, about three metres long. The thongs make a swaying, underwater forest. At the end of summer, they produce spores before the autumn gales rip them from the rock and they are washed up along the tide-line, like heaps of spaghetti.

Thong-weed buttons. Spot the ones begining to grow

Thong-weed, saw wrack and centre, oar-weed

Thong-weed floating as the tide rises

Among and below the thong-weed lies another, even thicker forest; arching, rubbery stems from which spread leathery fingers, like giants' hands, two metres long. This is the oar-weed, kelp or tangle-weed forest. The fronds swirl from side to side in the swell. Most of the forest is common oar-weed but there will be some furbelows, which has a knobbly, hollow holdfast and a wavy, pleated edge to the first part of the stem (a furbelows is a wavy edge). Furbelows, like thong-weed, is short-lived, and masses are washed up each autumn. My favourite oar-weed is sea-belt, a single, rippling frond that some children call 'crocodile-tail weed'.

You may find blue-rayed limpets browsing on the fronds of the oar-weeds. When young they are almost transparent and streaked with three, iridescent blue rays.

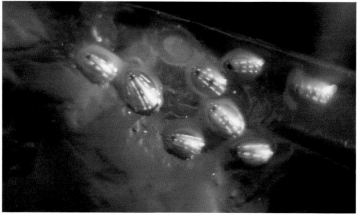

Blue-rayed limpets feeding on oar-weed

Oar-weeds floating with saw wrack

You will certainly see grey, lacy patches spreading on the fronds and stems of the oar-weeds. These are sea-mats, colonies made up of a honeycomb of cells, side by side, and each occupied by a tiny animal, although the colony operates as one organism. They are known as bryozoans, which means 'moss animals'. In summer the colonies spread at several millimetres a day, which is good news for the sea-slugs that feast on them. Other species of sea-mat grow on different seaweeds, especially saw-wrack and the carragheen 'mosses'.

The root-like holdfasts of the oar-weeds provide a home for many plants and animals. The greenleaf worm is one of this community. The little sea urchin *Psammechinus miliaris* may be found here; it camouflages itself by attaching pieces of weed to its spines. It is an omnivore, grazing on the seaweeds and on young barnacles and small molluscs, such as blue-rayed limpets.

Sea-urchin Psamechinus on oar-weed

Greenleaf worm

Sea belt on right and oar-weed, showing holdfasts, a skin of purple rock-weed and carragheen moss (Mastocarpus)

In the gullies, down on the lower shore, there are often boulders. Very gently lift one of these boulders. Having glimpsed some of its secrets, lower it back into the same position taking the greatest care, for most of the creatures which hide beneath the boulders are very fragile. When you first look at the underside of a boulder , it may appear barren. Look more carefully and you will see many, well-camouflaged animals, pressed close to the rock. There are brittle stars, with a small disc from which extend five, sinuous arms. Cushion stars are usually pale green, in the shape of five-cornered cushions with the corners slightly extended. The common starfish lives below low tide mark but is sometimes seen between the tides.

The broad-clawed porcelain crab can be common on the undersides of boulders. Its hairy, brown body and claws are flattened and its long feelers are swept back over its shell or carapace. Broad-clawed porcelain crabs are very delicate, hence the name 'porcelain'. Both on and under the boulders, side-shrimps (related to the sandhoppers along the tide-line) are often common.

Around and beneath the boulders may be grey topshells and a few of the tall, pointed, painted topshells. Sometimes a hermit crab will have taken over the shell. If you wait long enough, he will come out of his shell; first his eyes on stalks, then his lobster claws and finally his legs, to carry himself and his home scuttling for safety.

Under the boulders is a frequent hiding place for a squat lobster. They can give you a sharp nip with their long, slender pincers.

Brittle-star — now you see it now you don't

Crabs' pincers are even more effective and learning the technique of picking up a crab by spreading your fingers and thumb behind its pincers, without being nipped, is chief among the skills of a seasoned rock pooler! Shore crabs are easily the most common. Sometimes you find one 'in berry', with a granular mass of eggs under its 'tail'. Female shore crabs have wide 'tails' with seven segments, while male crabs have narrow 'tails' with only five segments.

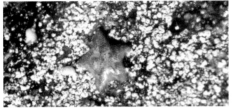

Cushion star with spiral tube-worms

Common starfish on Mastocarpus-carragheen moss

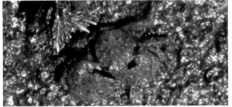

Broad-clawed porcelain crab, some camouflage!

Edible crabs, with brick-red shells, indented round the edge like a pie-crust may be hiding under the boulders. Less frequent are the furrowed crab and the hairy crab. Occasionally there may be a young spider crab, with their distinctive triangular, spiny carapace often disguised with fragments of seaweed.

Hermit crab inside a painted topshell

Squat lobster on green gut-weed

Female shore crab in 'berry'

But the most impressive crab of all is the fiddler or velvet swimming crab. It has startling red eyes and, when disturbed, opens its claws as if to take up a violin bow, or take a nip out of the finger of the first person to try to pick it up. The back legs are flattened and have a hairy fringe, especially adapted for swimming. They have beautiful violet-blue markings, like paint on a Maori warrior, and if you dare to gently stroke their back with one finger, it is as silky smooth as velvet.

On the undersides of some of the biggest boulders and on the walls of the deep gullies near low water, you will find some of our distant relatives – star ascidians. Star ascidians are colonial sea-squirts, each ray of each silver star is an individual animal but they act together, as a single organism. Sea-squirts begin life in the sea, as minute, tadpole-like larvae in the plankton and at that stage they, like us, possess an embryonic backbone – a notochord. When they settle on the rocks and develop their bodies of spreading jelly they lose their tail and notochord – their miraculous evolution has taken one direction and ours another.

Edible crab

Furrowed crab with a few spiral tube worms

Hairy crab

Velvet swimming crab with carragheen moss

Cowries, the spotted and unspotted species, are so small their scientific name is *Trivia* but they are not trivial for the star ascidians. Cowries feed almost exclusively on star ascidians. They even lay their eggs in the jelly, so the young hatch surrounded by food.

In sandy gullies near low tide, search for dahlia anemones. These anemones cover their sticky bodies with sand, giving them excellent camouflage, until the tide begins to rise and they spread their tentacles and then look like underwater dahlia flowers.

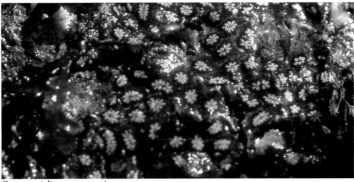
Star ascidian-sea-squirt

Sand-mason worms also cover themselves, even their tentacles, in sand. They spread their tentacles out beyond the sandy covering to catch the plankton drifting by. Sand mason worms are common on any sandy shore, not just in the sandy gullies.

Spotted cowrie, upper and lower sides

Dahlia anemones cover themselves with sand

Sand mason worms and grey topshell

To find fish under boulders or thick seaweed is one of the greatest excitements of rock pooling. There is a sudden threshing of fish-tail and a squeal of delight from the fisher. The worm pipe-fish is a fascinating creature. At first sight it does resemble a rather inflexible worm but a careful look at the snub-nosed snout shows it is related to the seahorse. The male, not the female, incubates the eggs.

The butterfish or gunnel might be mistaken for an eel but it has a series of about twelve dark spots along the back. It threshes vigorously when disturbed and is as slippery as butter.

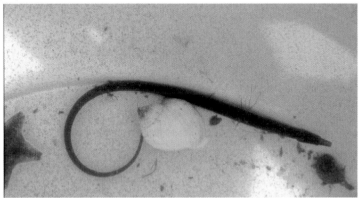

Worm pipe-fish. Can you see half a cushion-star?

Butterfish or gunnel

Another eel-like fish is the five-bearded rockling, which is a handsome reddish-brown with five barbels on its nose – the 'cat's whiskers' of a fish. Although smaller, the most strange and striking of the fish found under boulders is the Cornish sucker fish. It too is reddish in colour but with two blue spots, like extra eyes behind its real ones. With its sucker, it clings to the rock and its head is the same shape as a miniature, flattened, bottle-nosed dolphin.

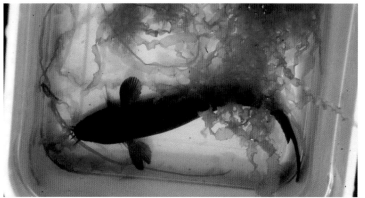

Five-bearded rockling with sea lettuce

Two Cornish sucker-fish

If you put on snorkel and mask and swim along among the weeds at low-tide you can see shoals of sand-eels; silver arrows, shooting through the oarweed forest and suddenly disappearing into a patch of sand. You may find these too in the biggest rock pools and in the big, sandy pools at Bantham. The oarweed forest just below low-tide is also the home of the Ballan wrasse; green and red, they swim, in almost tropical splendour in and out of the gullies and swaying weeds. Male wrasse, like sticklebacks, build nests for their mates. They are also remarkable in being able to start life as females and in later life change into males.

As you look down, you may see a big jellyfish, like this *Cyanea*, pulsing though the clear water beside you, a reminder that all life from jellyfish to humankind owes its beginnings to the sea.

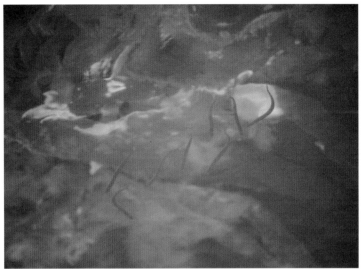

Sand eels in a 'gaint's bath' rockpool

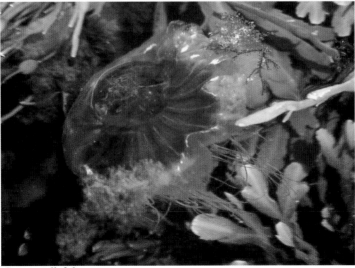

Cyanea jellyfish

SHELL COLLECTING

Walk along the beach near high tideline and you will find shells. Make sure they are empty, for often shells are washed up with their owner still inside, dead or alive. Don't take these home, they will soon announce their presence with an unpleasant smell. Collecting empty seashells is a fascinating and addictive pastime. You can look for a special variety, like the tiny cowries, or you can collect one of each species, or collect a mixture and display them as an artistic creation. You might make a display in an old shoe box, using tissue paper for water and weeds. You can also make shell necklaces and shell earrings

The shells washed up along the pebbly beaches of Hallsands, Beesands, Torcross, Slapton and Blackpool are different from most of the other beaches, so we have made a separate list for them. Sometimes you may find very few shells, sometimes masses but half of the fun is in the looking.

There are many games you can make up while collecting shells. Shell Monopoly is one. Give each shell a value (I have suggested some below, by the list of shells you are likely to find) and try to collect as many as ten of each shell in a set time – perhaps ten minutes. At the end of the time compare your beautiful finds and count up your shell money to see who has 'won'.

Suggested shell Monopoly prices

Shell list for most beaches		Shell list for Hallsands, Beesands, Torcross, Slapton and Blackpool Sands	
Cowrie	£10		
Blue-rayed limpet	£5		
Thick-lipped dog-whelk	£2		
Netted dog-whelk	£1	Pelican's foot	£10
Dog-whelk	50p	Necklace shell	£5
Sting winkle	£1	Turban topshell	£2
Painted topshell	£1	Whelk	£1
Turban topshell	50p	Slipper limpet	50p
Thick topshell	20p	Mussel	20p
Grey topshell	20p	Limpet	10p
Purple topshell	10p	Trough shell	5p
Cockle	10p		
Mussel	10p		
Rough winkle	20p		
Flat winkle	20p		
Edible winkle	10p		
Limpet	5p		

Shingle beaches: *Hallsands, Beesands, Torcross, Slapton, Blackpool Sands*
1. Limpet. 2. Razor. 3. Whelk. 4. Hornwrack. 5. Mussel. 6. Slipper limpet. 7. Turban topshell.
8. Necklace shell. 9. Trough shell 10. Cockle. 11. Pelican's foot shell

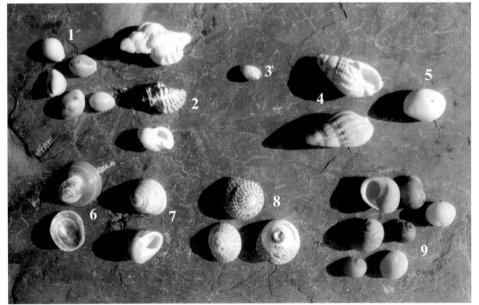

Most beaches
1. Cowries. 2. Sting Winkle. 3. Thick - lipped dog - whelk. 4. Netted dog - whelk.
5. Dog - whelk. 6. Blue - rayed limpet. 7. Grey topshell 8. Purple topshell. 9. Flat Winkle.

SEAWEEDS

These are photocopies, about 25% life-size, of actual seaweeds floated onto white paper. The delicate seaweeds make beautiful designs when floated onto paper or thin card and make lovely cards. Use a soft paintbrush to arrange the frond artistically. Do not pick the living seaweeds but take those that have been washed up or broken off; you will often find some along the tideline or floating in rock pools. Wash the weeds in a bowl of sea water first, so that you can return any little creatures, that swim out of the weed, into a rock pool.

To name them can be difficult, but preserved like this the seaweeds will remain things of beauty that will last forever.

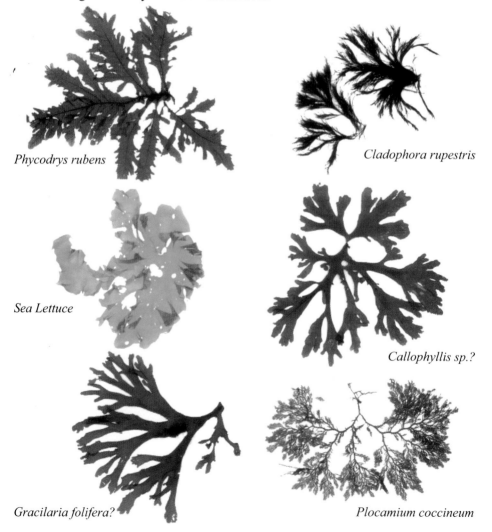

Phycodrys rubens

Cladophora rupestris

Sea Lettuce

Callophyllis sp.?

Gracilaria folifera?

Plocamium coccineum